Kids can cook!

Nicola Graimes

Love Food ® is an imprint of Parragon Books Ltd

Parragon
Queen Street House
4 Queen Street
Bath BA1 1HE, UK

ISBN: 978-1-4075-3392-6

Printed in China

Written by Nicola Graimes
Photography by Mike Cooper
Food styling by Lincoln Jefferson
Designed by Seamonster Design

With a special thank you to Ruby, Harvey, Jacob, Matthew, Asia, Gabrielle, Giselle,
Nikki, and Chris.

Notes for the Reader

This book uses imperial, metric, and U.S. cup measurements. Follow the same units of
measurement throughout; do not mix imperial and metric. All spoon measurements are
level: teaspoons are assumed to be 5 ml, and tablespoons are assumed to be 15 ml.
Unless otherwise stated, milk is assumed to be whole, eggs and individual vegetables,
such as potatoes, are medium, and pepper is freshly ground black pepper.

The times given are an approximate guide only. Preparation times differ according to the
techniques used by different people, and the cooking times may also vary from those
given as a result of the type of oven used. Optional ingredients, variations, or serving
suggestions have not been included in the calculations.

Recipes using raw or very lightly cooked eggs should be avoided by infants, the elderly,
pregnant women, convalescents, and anyone with a chronic condition. Pregnant and
breastfeeding women are advised to avoid eating peanuts and peanut products. People
who have nut allergies should be aware that some of the prepared ingredients used in the
recipes in this book may contain nuts. Always check the packaging before use.

Contents

Cooking together

Cooking is fun and it's even more fun if you can do it with someone else. All the recipes in this book have been created for you—the "top chef"—to cook with an adult—the "kitchen assistant"—with a lot of delicious results. Cooking is all about fun, learning, and experimenting, and there are plenty of ideas here for you to try, from breakfasts and lunches to dinners and desserts. Get your family and friends to give you marks out of 10 and add your thoughts on the recipes to the Recipe record charts!

Before you start...

There are a few important rules to remember when you are cooking. The following tips will make sure your recipes taste great and work every time.

1 Read the recipe before you start. Try to get all your ingredients ready and make sure you have the equipment listed.

2 Wash your hands before you start cooking, put an apron on to protect your clothes, and tie your hair back if it is long.

3 For successful results, be careful when measuring your ingredients. Make sure dry ingredients are even. Put liquids in a measuring cup on an even surface, bending down so that your eye will be even with the markings on the cup when measuring.

Cooking tips

Using the recipes

The recipes in this book are graded with stars, meaning that some are more difficult than others:

★ = easy

★ ★ = a little tricky

★ ★ ★ = a little more challenging

The recipes also have symbols to help you. Look out for:

 Serves/Makes

Preparation time

Cooking time

Safe cooking!

- Always ask an adult first before starting to cook and be especially careful when handling anything hot, sharp, or electrical.

- Always wear oven mitts when handling hot baking sheets, pans, and dishes.

- When stirring food in a pan, hold the handle firmly to keep it steady.

- Turn pan handles to the side, away from the heat, so they aren't accidentally knocked off the stovetop.

- Wipe up any spills on the floor to prevent slipping.

- Do not walk around the kitchen with a sharp knife in your hand. Always ask an adult before you use a knife.

- Remember to switch off the stovetop or oven when you have finished cooking.

Clean up

- Always wash your hands thoroughly before you start to cook and after handling raw meat and fish.

- Use separate cutting boards for vegetables and meat. If this is not possible, make sure they are washed thoroughly between uses.

- Store raw and cooked food separately in the refrigerator.

- Make sure that the ingredients you use have not passed their expiration date.

- Wipe down work surfaces after use and make sure everything is clean and tidy.

If you see the ❗ symbol, it means you need to ask an adult to help you. This could be because a hot oven, stovetop, electrical appliance, sharp knife, or scissors are involved in the recipe preparation.

How to...

Here are some useful cooking words and terms:

Grating cheese

Hold the cheese against a grater and rub it up and down over the large holes to make coarse shreds—keep your fingers out of the way.

Separating eggs

Crack the egg, pull open the shell with your fingers, and let it plop into a bowl. Put an eggcup over the yolk and pour the white into another bowl.

Rubbing in

When making pastry, mix or rub the butter into the flour with your fingertips until the mixture resembles fine breadcrumbs.

Rolling out dough

Lightly flour the surface and rolling pin, then roll out the dough away from you in gentle movements, turning it occasionally, until it makes a thin sheet.

Whipping

To add air to cream or egg whites, beat them with a whisk until they firm up and form peaks.

Creaming

To add air to cakes, beat the butter and sugar together with a whisk or wooden spoon until they are light and creamy in texture.

Melting chocolate

Put the bowl of chocolate pieces over a pan of gently simmering water—make sure the bowl does not touch the water—until melted.

Cooking pasta/noodles

Put the pasta/noodles in a large pan of boiling salted water. Cook the pasta/noodles in the boiling water, stirring occasionally, until just tender.

Essential equipment

1 saucepans

2 colander

3 cake pan

4 muffin pan

5 baking sheet

6 mixing bowl

7 strainer

8 measuring cup

9 lemon juicer

10 rolling pin

11 oven mitts

12 cooling rack

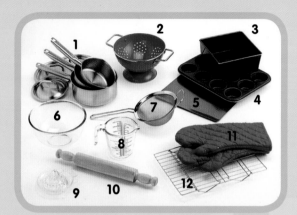

1 electric blender

2 weighing scales

3 food processor

4 grater

5 tongs

6 handheld electric mixer

7 beaters

8 storage container

9 handheld electric blender

10 balloon whisk

1 measuring cups

2 pastry brush

3 flour sifter

4 plastic spatula

5 slotted spoon

6 metal spatula

7 scissors

8 sharp knives

9 cutting board

10 garlic press

11 cookie cutter

12 vegetable peeler

13 wooden skewers

14 wooden spoon

15 wooden spatula

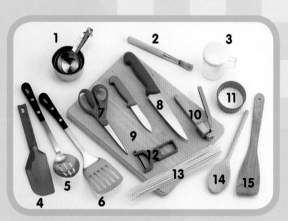

Recipe record chart

Recipe	Date cooked	who for?	Marks out of 10

Recipe record chart

Recipe	Date cooked	who for?	Marks out of 10

Recipe record chart

Recipe	Date cooked	Who for?	Marks out of 10

Recipe record chart

Recipe	Date cooked	Who for?	Marks out of 10

Great start

Breakfast is one of the most important meals because it helps to give your body a lot of energy for the day ahead. Ask your mom, dad, or another adult to help you treat the rest of the family to one of these delicious ways to start the day—there's plenty to choose from, such as a rich and creamy smoothie, crunchy honey-oat cereal, scrumptious pancakes, and, for a weekend treat, a big eggs and bacon breakfast.

Sunrise crush and Going bananas ★

Bring a ray of sunshine to your day with these tropical juices that are brimming with goodness. If making juice in a blender, you may want to press it through a strainer to make it smooth.

Serves 4

prep: 10 minutes

cooking: none

What you need:

Sunrise crush
1 medium ripe pineapple
5 oranges, halved
ice cubes, to serve

Going bananas
1 large ripe mango
4 bananas, peeled and cut into chunks
1¾ cups plain yogurt
1¾ cups coconut milk

Equipment:
- sharp knife
- cutting board
- electric juicer, blender, or food processor
- mixing bowl
- large pitcher
- tablespoon

Step 1: ❗

To make "Sunrise crush," slice off the bottom of the pineapple and stand it upright on a board. Remove the spiky skin, then cut into six long pieces.

Step 2: ❗

Puree the pineapple in the electric juicer, blender, or food processor.

Step 3:

Squeeze the oranges, then mix the orange and pineapple juices together in a pitcher. Pour the juice into 4 glasses. Top with some ice cubes.

Step 1: ❗

To make "Going bananas," cut both sides of the mango away from the pit in the middle. Scoop out the flesh with a spoon.

Step 2: ❗

Slice the bananas into chunks and place in the electric juicer, blender, or food processor with the mango, yogurt, and coconut milk. Put on the lid and blend until smooth.

Step 3:

Pour the smoothie into 4 glasses. Serve with straws.

marks out of 10

10=yummylicious **9**=truly scrumptious
8=de-lovely **7**=delicious
6=tasty **5**=Mmmmmmm
4=mouthwatering **3**=just nice
2=good **1**=ok

. . . . ✓

15

Breakfast oatmeal **

Just the thing to warm you up on a cold winter's morning, this creamy oatmeal is topped with a cinnamon apple puree, maple syrup, and a sprinkling of pecan nuts.

Serves 4

prep: 15 minutes

cooking: 15 minutes

What you need:

2½ cups rolled oats

3¼ cups milk

3¼ cups water

8 pecan nuts, to serve (optional)

maple syrup, to serve

Cinnamon apple puree:

4 apples

1 tsp lemon juice

¾ cup water

½–1 tsp ground cinnamon

Equipment:

- vegetable peeler
- sharp knife
- cutting board
- fork
- small and large saucepans with lids
- large spoon

Step 1: ❗

To make the puree, remove the skin from the apples, using a vegetable peeler. Cut the apple into quarters, remove the core, then cut the flesh into small pieces.

Step 2: ❗

Put the apple pieces, lemon juice, water, and cinnamon in a small saucepan. Cover and simmer for 15 minutes, until the apples are soft.

Step 3: ❗

While the apple mixture is cooking, put the oats in a large saucepan with the milk and water, then bring to a boil.

Step 4: ❗

When the oat mixture is bubbling, reduce the heat to low; half cover the pan with a lid, and simmer for 8 minutes, stirring frequently.

Step 5:

Mash the apple with a fork until mushy. Spoon the creamy oatmeal into 4 bowls, then top each one with apple puree.

Step 6:

Add the pecans, if using, and drizzle over the maple syrup. Try arranging the nuts and syrup in a fun pattern, as shown on page 16.

marks out of 10

10=yummylicious **9**=truly scrumptious
8=de-lovely **7**=delicious
6=tasty **5**=Mmmmmmm
4=mouthwatering **3**=just nice
2=good **1**=ok

. . . .

Golden nuggets ★★

This golden, crunchy breakfast cereal will give you plenty of energy. It's great served with milk or yogurt and topped with your favorite fresh fruit.

Makes about 10 portions

prep: 15 minutes

cooking: 28 minutes

What you need:

½ cup whole almonds, with skins removed

2½ cups rolled oats

scant ½ cup sesame seeds

scant ½ cup sunflower seeds

scant ½ cup pumpkin seeds

3 tbsp sunflower oil

8 tbsp honey

½ cup shelled walnuts, roughly broken

heaping ½ cup raisins

To serve:

your favorite fresh fruit, such as raspberries, sliced strawberries, bananas, or nectarines

milk or natural yogurt

Equipment:

• large mixing bowl

• wooden spoon

• small saucepan

• 2 baking sheets

Step 1: (!)

Turn the oven on to 275°F/140°C. Put the almonds, oats, and seeds in a large mixing bowl.

Step 2: (!)

Put the oil and honey in a small saucepan and, over a medium heat, stir until melted and mixed together.

Step 3:

Pour the honey mixture into the mixing bowl and stir well with a wooden spoon, until the nuts, oats, and seeds are coated.

Step 4: (!)

Spoon the oat mixture onto 2 baking sheets in an even layer and bake for 15 minutes; then mix in the walnuts.

Step 5: (!)

Cook the oat mixture for another 10 minutes, until golden. (The mixture will become crisp as it cools.)

Step 6:

Put the cereal in a mixing bowl and stir in the raisins; let cool. Serve with milk or yogurt and top with fruit.

marks out of 10

10=yummylicious **9**=truly scrumptious
8=de-lovely **7**=delicious
6=tasty **5**=Mmmmmmm
4=mouthwatering **3**=just nice
2=good **1**=ok

. . . .

19

Perfect pancakes ★★

Your family and friends will love these light pancakes—they're so delicious that they'll disappear in seconds! They make a great afternoon treat, too.

Makes 16

prep: 10 minutes

cooking:
20 minutes

What you need:

1 cup self-rising flour

2 tbsp superfine sugar

1 large egg, lightly beaten

¾ cup milk

3 tbsp plain yogurt, plus extra
   to serve

2 tbsp unsalted butter, for frying

10 oz/275 g frozen mixed berries,
   defrosted

maple syrup, to serve

Equipment:

• strainer

• large mixing bowl

• pitcher

• wooden spoon

• large nonstick skillet

• spatula

Step 1:

Sift the flour into a mixing bowl. Stir in the sugar and make a dip in the center. Mix together the egg and milk in a pitcher.

Step 2:

Pour the milk mixture into the flour. Add the yogurt and stir with a wooden spoon until you have a smooth batter.

Step 3: ❗

Melt a quarter of the butter in a skillet. Add 3 spoonfuls of batter to make 3 pancakes, each one about 2½ inches/ 6 cm in diameter.

Step 4: ❗

Cook for 2 minutes, until bubbles appear on the top of the pancake and the underneath is golden. Flip each pancake over and cook for another minute.

Step 5: ❗

Repeat with the rest of the batter to make about 16 pancakes. Add a little more butter when the skillet looks dry.

Step 6:

Serve the pancakes with a large spoonful of fruit and yogurt and drizzle over the maple syrup.

marks out of 10

10=yummylicious **9**=truly scrumptious
8=de-lovely **7**=delicious
6=tasty **5**=Mmmmmmm
4=mouthwatering **3**=just nice
2=good **1**=ok

. . . .

21

Big breakfast ★★

Treat your family to a special weekend breakfast or brunch with this hearty meal of egg, bacon, potato cakes, and tomatoes.

Serves 4

prep: 15 minutes

cooking: 20 minutes

what you need:

1 lb/450 g large potatoes, peeled

5 eggs

3 tbsp all-purpose flour

3 tbsp sunflower oil

8 slices bacon

6 cherry tomatoes, halved, to serve (optional)

salt and pepper

Equipment:

- grater
- sharp knife
- cutting board
- mixing bowl
- large skillet
- spatula
- paper towels
- small bowl

Step 1:

Grate the potatoes, rinse in a strainer, then lay them on a dish towel. Gather up the sides and squeeze to remove any water.

Step 2: (!)

Turn on the broiler to medium–high. Put the potatoes in a bowl with 1 beaten egg and the flour; season and stir.

Step 3: (!)

Heat 2 tbsp of the oil in a skillet. Take a handful of the potato mixture and form into patties, about 2¾ inches/ 7 cm across.

Step 4: (!)

Put 3 potato cakes in the pan and cook each side for about 5 minutes, until golden; drain on paper towels and make 3 more.

Step 5: (!)

Meanwhile, broil the bacon for 8 minutes, turning once, until crisp. Broil the tomatoes either side for a few minutes, if using. Crack an egg into a bowl, then slide into the pan.

Step 6: (!)

Repeat with the rest of the eggs and cook for 5 minutes, until the white is set. Serve with the bacon, potato cakes, and tomatoes.

marks out of 10

10=yummylicious **9**=truly scrumptious
8=de-lovely **7**=delicious
6=tasty **5**=Mmmmmmm
4=mouthwatering **3**=just nice
2=good **1**=ok

. . . . ✓

Super snacks

Feeling hunger pangs? Ask your kitchen assistant to help you make these tasty appetite quenchers. There are ideas for all kinds of occasions, from a movie night at home, to party treats and lunch-box fillers. Some of these recipes would also make a great lunch served with a salad or a selection of crunchy vegetable sticks.

Roll up, roll up! ★

This yummy roll is extra special because it has a secret layer of delicious pesto.

Makes 1

prep: 10 minutes

cooking: none

What you need:

1 large crusty roll

1 tsp prepared green pesto

1 tbsp mayonnaise

2 slices ham or cooked chicken

2 crisp lettuce leaves

1 oz/30 g cheese, cut into thin slices

4 thin, round slices cucumber

Equipment:

• sharp knife

• cutting board

• spoon

• bowl

• plastic wrap

Step 1: ❗

Slice off the top of the roll to form a lid and use a spoon to scoop out the soft bread from the inside to make a hollow.

Step 2:

Mix together the pesto and mayonnaise in a bowl and spread it all over the inside of the roll and the lid.

Step 3:

Fold one of the slices of ham or chicken, then place it in the bottom of the roll. Top with the lettuce.

Step 4:

Next, add the remaining slice of ham or chicken and top with a layer of cheese.

Step 5:

Now add the cucumber, then press the filling down slightly and top with the roll "lid."

Step 6:

The roll can be eaten right away or wrapped in plastic wrap and stored in the refrigerator for a few hours.

marks out of 10

10=yummylicious **9**=truly scrumptious
8=de-lovely **7**=delicious
6=tasty **5**=Mmmmmmm
4=mouthwatering **3**=just nice
2=good **1**=ok

. . . . ✓

27

Poptastic ★★

Lots of fun to make and just as tasty to eat, popcorn is the perfect snack!

Serves 4

prep: 5 minutes

cooking:
5 minutes

What you need:

- 1–2 tbsp vegetable oil
- ¼ cup uncooked popcorn kernels
- 1 tbsp butter
- 3 tbsp maple syrup
- 1 tbsp sesame seeds

Equipment:

- medium-size saucepan with lid
- large mixing bowl
- small saucepan
- wooden spoon

Step 1: ❗

Pour the vegetable oil into a saucepan—it should cover the bottom of the pan. Heat the oil over a medium heat.

Step 2: ❗

Carefully add the popcorn kernels to the pan in an even layer and cover with a lid; a glass lid is best so you can see into the pan.

Step 3: ❗

Cook the popcorn over a medium–low heat, shaking the pan occasionally, until the popcorn kernels pop.

Step 4: ❗

Pour the popcorn into a large mixing bowl, discarding any kernels that have not popped.

Step 5: ❗

Melt the butter in a small saucepan, then pour in the maple syrup. Bring to a boil, then remove from the heat and cool.

Step 6: ❗

Pour the maple syrup sauce over the popcorn, add the sesame seeds, and stir to mix together. Now it is ready to serve!

marks out of 10

10=yummylicious **9**=truly scrumptious
8=de-lovely **7**=delicious
6=tasty **5**=Mmmmmmm
4=mouthwatering **3**=just nice
2=good **1**=ok

. . . . ✓

Cinnamon raisin French toast★★

This delicious snack would also make a great breakfast served with yogurt and fruit, or try it as a dessert with your favorite ice cream. You could also use sliced bread, English muffins, or brioche instead.

Serves 4

prep: 5 minutes

cooking:
10 minutes

What you need:

3 large eggs
8 tbsp milk
1 tsp ground cinnamon
2 tbsp superfine sugar
1 tbsp sunflower oil
1½-2 tbsp unsalted butter
4 slices raisin bread

Equipment:

• shallow dish
• fork or whisk
• large skillet

Step 1:

Crack the eggs into a shallow dish and pour in the milk. Lightly beat with a fork or whisk until combined.

Step 2:

Next, add half the cinnamon and half the superfine sugar to the egg mixture and stir or whisk until mixed in.

Step 3: ❗

Put half of the oil and butter in a large skillet. Warm over a medium–low heat until the butter has melted.

Step 4: ❗

Swirl the butter and oil around the skillet. Dip the raisin bread into the egg mixture until both sides are coated.

Step 5: ❗

Put two slices of the bread in the pan and cook for 2 minutes on each side, until golden. Keep warm.

Step 6: ❗

Heat the rest of the oil and butter in the skillet. Prepare and cook the rest of the bread. Mix together the remaining sugar and cinnamon, sprinkle over the toast, and serve.

marks out of 10

10=yummylicious **9**=truly scrumptious
8=de-lovely **7**=delicious
6=tasty **5**=Mmmmmmm
4=mouthwatering **3**=just nice
2=good **1**=ok

. . . . ✔

It's a wrap! ★★

These golden tortilla wraps are delicious as a light lunch served with vegetable sticks. They are filled with chopped tomato, tuna, and melted mozzarella, but you can also try pesto, chicken, or ham.

Serves 2

prep: 5 minutes

cooking: 4 minutes

what you need:

6 tbsp canned tuna, drained
2 soft flour tortillas
2 small tomatoes
8 slices mozzarella
2 tsp sunflower oil
salt and pepper

Equipment:

- small bowl
- fork
- sharp knife
- teaspoon
- cutting board
- skillet
- spatula

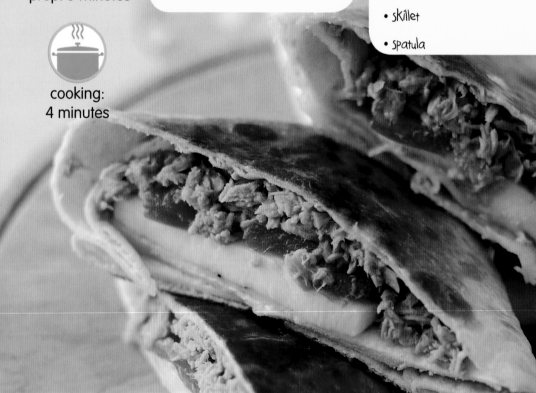

Step 1:

Put the tuna in a bowl and mash with a fork. Spoon the tuna onto the center of the tortillas.

Step 2: !

Cut the tomatoes in half, scoop out the seeds using a teaspoon, then throw away the seeds. Cut the tomatoes into small pieces.

Step 3:

Sprinkle the tomatoes on the tuna, then place the mozzarella on top. Season the filling with salt and pepper.

Step 4:

Carefully fold in the sides, then the ends of the tortillas to make 2 square-shaped wraps.

Step 5: !

Heat the oil in a skillet and put the wraps in it, folded-side down.

Step 6: !

Cook the wraps for about 4 minutes over a medium–low heat, turning once, until golden. Cut each diagonally in half before serving.

marks out of 10

10=yummylicious 9=truly scrumptious
8=de-lovely 7=delicious
6=tasty 5=Mmmmmmm
4=mouthwatering 3=just nice
2=good 1=ok

. . . .

Cheese sticks ★★★

These golden cheese sticks are so good they just melt in the mouth. They not only make a tasty after-school snack but are great party or picnic food, too.

Makes 16

prep: 10 minutes

cooking:
10 minutes

What you need:

¾ cup all-purpose flour, plus extra
  for dusting
½ tsp paprika (optional)
3 tbsp butter, plus extra for greasing
scant ¾ cup grated Parmesan cheese
1 egg, lightly beaten

Equipment:

- 2 baking sheets
- strainer
- mixing bowl
- rolling pin
- wire cooling rack

Step 1: ❗

Turn the oven on to 400°F/200°C. Lightly grease 2 baking sheets with butter.

Step 2:

Sift the flour and the paprika, if using, into a mixing bowl. Cut the butter into pieces, then add to the bowl.

Step 3:

Rub the butter into the flour with your fingertips until the mixture looks like breadcrumbs. Stir in the Parmesan cheese.

Step 4:

Stir the egg into the bowl with a fork, then use your hands to form the dough into a ball.

Step 5: ❗

Roll out the dough on a floured surface until ¼ inch/ 5 mm thick. Trim the edges. Cut into 16 ½-inch/1-cm wide x 4-inch/10-cm long strips.

Step 6: ❗

Put the cheese sticks, spaced apart, on the baking sheets and cook for 10 minutes, until golden. Cool on a wire rack.

marks out of 10

10=yummylicious 9=truly scrumptious
8=de-lovely 7=delicious
6=tasty 5=Mmmmmmm
4=mouthwatering 3=just nice
2=good 1=ok

. . . . ✓

Meals in minutes

Treat your friends and family to these quick and simple ideas for lunch and dinner. There's something for everyone here, with recipes influenced by dishes from different countries, such as Italian spaghetti with meatballs, tasty Chinese noodles with chicken nuggets, and Mexican-style tortilla baskets filled with a lightly spiced bean stew.

Sunset soup ★★

You can use pumpkin instead of squash for this delicious and nutritious soup.

Serves 4

prep: 15 minutes

cooking:
30 minutes

What you need:

2lb 4 oz/1 kg butternut squash

1 tbsp olive oil

1 large onion, sliced

1 celery stalk, sliced

1 leek, sliced

1 large carrot, sliced

5 cups vegetable stock

2 bay leaves

1 bouquet garni

1 tsp dried thyme

salt and pepper

grated sharp cheddar cheese
   and crusty bread, to serve

Equipment:

• sharp knife

• cutting board

• large saucepan with lid

• spoon

• handheld electric blender

• ladle

• grater

Step 1: ⚠

Cut the squash into thick slices, then cut off the skin. Scoop out the seeds with a spoon and cut into chunks.

Step 2: ⚠

Heat the oil in a saucepan and fry the onion for 5 minutes, then add the squash, celery, leek, and carrot; stir well.

Step 3: ⚠

Cook the vegetables for 3 minutes with the lid on. Pour in the stock and add the bay leaves, bouquet garni, and thyme.

Step 4: ⚠

Bring the soup to a boil, then reduce the heat and simmer, half covered, for 20 minutes, until the vegetables are tender.

Step 5: ⚠

Remove the pan from the heat and, using a handheld electric blender, blend the soup until smooth. Season with salt and pepper.

Step 6: ⚠

Ladle the soup into bowls and top with a sprinkling of grated cheese. Serve with crusty bread.

marks out of 10

10=yummylicious 9=truly scrumptious
8=de-lovely 7=delicious
6=tasty 5=Mmmmmmm
4=mouthwatering 3=just nice
2=good 1=ok

. . . . ✔

Salmon bites ★★

These golden, crispy balls of potato and brain-boosting salmon taste great and go well with the creamy dipping sauce.

Serves 4

prep: 20 minutes, plus chilling

cooking: 25 minutes

What you need:

2 x 7½ oz/213 g cans salmon, skin and large bones removed

1 lb 6 oz/630 g potatoes, peeled, cooked and cooled

1 small egg, beaten

flour, for coating

3 tbsp sunflower oil

salt and pepper

lemon wedges, to serve

Dipping sauce:

4 tbsp mayonnaise

2 tbsp tartar sauce

2 tbsp olive oil

1 tsp fresh lemon juice

Equipment:

• large mixing bowl

• grater

• spoon

• plate

• large skillet

• spatula

• small mixing bowl

Step 1:

Put the salmon in a large bowl. Using your hands, flake the fish into chunks.

Step 2:

Grate the potatoes into the bowl with the salmon. Stir in the egg, salt, and pepper. Cover the bowl and chill for 30 minutes.

Step 3:

Thickly cover a plate with flour. Take one spoonful of the salmon mixture at a time, about the size of a golf ball.

Step 4:

Using floured hands, shape the salmon mixture to make 16 balls, then dip each of the balls in the flour until lightly coated.

Step 5: !

Heat the oil in a skillet and fry half of the balls for 10 minutes, turning, until golden. Repeat with the remaining balls.

Step 6:

Drain the balls on paper towels. Mix together the ingredients for the sauce, then serve with the salmon balls and lemon wedges.

marks out of 10

10=yummylicious **9**=truly scrumptious
8=de-lovely **7**=delicious
6=tasty **5**=Mmmmmmm
4=mouthwatering **3**=just nice
2=good **1**=ok

. . . . ✔

41

Chicken nuggets with loads of noodles★★

Fresh, fast, and healthy, this recipe makes a perfect lunch or dinner to treat your friends and family.

serves 4

prep: 20 minutes, plus marinating

cooking: 15 minutes

What you need:

4 skinless chicken breasts, 5 oz/ 150 g each, cut into ½ inch/1 cm cubes

9 oz/250 g medium egg noodles

2 scallions, peeled and finely chopped

1 tbsp sesame seeds (optional)

Marinade:

4 tbsp soy sauce

2 tbsp toasted sesame oil

2 tbsp honey

2-inch/5-cm piece fresh ginger, peeled and sliced

2 large cloves garlic, peeled and sliced

Equipment:

• shallow medium-size dish

• sharp knife

• cutting board

• large spoon

• shallow dish

• plastic wrap

• foil

• wooden skewers soaked in water until ready to use

• medium saucepan

• strainer

Step 1:

For the marinade, mix together all the ingredients in a shallow dish. Add the chicken pieces and turn until coated; cover with plastic wrap.

Step 2:

Chill, allowing the chicken to absorb the flavors of the marinade for at least 30 minutes, turning it occasionally.

Step 3: ❗

Turn on the broiler to high, or heat a ridged grill pan. Thread the chicken pieces onto 8 wooden skewers, place in the shallow dish and spoon over a little marinade.

Step 4: ❗

Broil or grill the chicken sticks for 4 minutes. Turn the sticks over, spoon over more marinade, then cook for another 4 minutes.

Step 5: ❗

Cook the noodles, following the package instructions. Pour the marinade through a strainer into a small pan and boil gently for 1 minute, stirring.

Step 6:

To serve, put the noodles and skewers onto 4 plates. Spoon the marinade over the noodles and sprinkle with scallions and sesame seeds (if using).

marks out of 10

10=yummylicious 9=truly scrumptious
8=de-lovely 7=delicious
6=tasty 5=Mmmmmmm
4=mouthwatering 3=just nice
2=good 1=ok

. . . . ✔

43

Mighty meatball spaghetti ★★★

Meatballs are always popular and these will be no exception. They come in a rich tomato sauce and are served on a bed of swirly spaghetti. Sprinkle some extra grated Parmesan cheese over the meatballs if you like.

serves 4

prep: 20 minutes

cooking:
30 minutes

what you need:

1½ oz/45 g crustless, day-old
  bread, broken into chunks
14 oz/400 g lean ground beef
2 cloves garlic, crushed
1 large egg, lightly beaten
heaping ¼ cup grated Parmesan cheese
flour, for coating
10½ oz/300 g dried spaghetti
salt and pepper

Tomato sauce:
2 tbsp olive oil
2 cloves garlic, crushed
2 tsp dried oregano
2 x 14 oz/400 g cans chopped tomatoes
1 tbsp tomato paste
1 tsp sugar

Equipment:
• food processor
• 2 large saucepans, one with lid
• large spoon
• colander

Step 1: ❗

Put the bread in a food processor and blend until it makes breadcrumbs. Add the beef, garlic, egg, Parmesan cheese, salt, and pepper.

Step 2: ❗

Process the beef mixture until it comes together in a ball. Flour your hands and roll the mixture into balls the size of walnuts.

Step 3: ❗

Chill the balls, then make the tomato sauce. Heat the oil in a saucepan and add the garlic and oregano. Stir for 1 minute.

Step 4: ❗

Add the chopped tomatoes, tomato paste, and sugar; bring to a boil, then reduce the heat and simmer for 8 minutes.

Step 5: ❗

Carefully place the meatballs in the pan and spoon the sauce over them. Cover and simmer for 20 minutes, turning the meatballs occasionally.

Step 6: ❗

Meanwhile, cook the pasta in a large pan of salted water, following the package instructions. Drain and serve with the meatballs and sauce.

marks out of 10

10=yummylicious **9**=truly scrumptious
8=de-lovely **7**=delicious
6=tasty **5**=Mmmmmmm
4=mouthwatering **3**=just nice
2=good **1**=ok

. . . . ✓

45

Mexican bean baskets ★★★

A tortilla makes the perfect basket shape when baked. Put a layer of crispy shredded lettuce in the basket if you want, then top with the bean stew. A spoonful of guacamole and grated cheese taste good, too.

Serves 4

prep: 15 minutes

cooking: 40 minutes

what you need:

2 tbsp olive oil, plus extra for brushing

2 onions, finely chopped

2 large cloves garlic, crushed

1 large red bell pepper, seeded and diced

2 zucchini, diced

3 tsp ground cumin

½ tsp ground cinnamon

2 tsp ground coriander

2 x 14 oz/400 g cans kidney beans, drained and rinsed

2 x 14 oz/400 g cans chopped tomatoes

2 tbsp ketchup

4 large, soft tortillas

salt and pepper

Equipment:

• sharp knife

• cutting board

• large saucepan with lid

• pastry brush

• 4 heatproof bowls

• large baking sheet

Step 1: ❗

Turn the oven on to 350°F/180°C. Heat the oil in a saucepan and add the onions. Stir to coat them in the oil.

Step 2: ❗

Cook the onions, with the lid on, for 8 minutes, stirring now and then. Stir in the garlic, red bell pepper, and zucchini.

Step 3: ❗

Next, add the spices and kidney beans, followed by the tomatoes and ketchup. Bring to a boil, then reduce the heat.

Step 4: ❗

Half cover the pan with a lid and simmer for 20 minutes, stirring every now and then. Season with salt and pepper.

Step 5:

Lightly brush the tortillas on both sides with oil. Place each one in a heatproof bowl, shaping the sides to make a basket.

Step 6: ❗

Place the bowls on a baking sheet and bake the tortillas for 9 minutes, until crisp. Let cool slightly and carefully remove from the bowls. Divide the beans between the "baskets."

marks out of 10

10=yummylicious **9**=truly scrumptious
8=de-lovely **7**=delicious
6=tasty **5**=Mmmmmmm
4=mouthwatering **3**=just nice
2=good **1**=ok

. . . . ✔

Sweet treats

Your kitchen assistant won't need much persuading to join you in making these scrumptious treats! You'll both have a lot of fun preparing yummy desserts, such as the toffee banana sundae or delicious apple pie. Try making jelly-filled cookies, decorating cupcakes with flowers and bugs, or make your own sparkly chocolate truffles—they make the perfect gift!

Very berry big mess*

Nothing could be simpler to make—or more delicious to eat—than this dessert with whipped vanilla cream, fresh strawberries, and chunks of chocolate cake.

Makes 4

prep: 15 minutes

cooking: none

what you need:

1 lb/450 g ripe strawberries, green part removed, halved or quartered

3 tbsp confectioners' sugar

1½ cups whipping cream

2 tsp vanilla extract

4 slices chocolate sponge loaf cake or brownies

Equipment:

- electric blender
- strainer
- spoon
- small and large mixing bowls
- whisk or handheld electric mixer
- wooden spoon

Step 1:

Put just under half of the strawberries in a blender. Blend until pureed, then press through a strainer to remove any seeds.

Step 2:

Put the rest of the strawberries in a bowl and sprinkle over 1 tbsp of the confectioners' sugar. Stir and set aside.

Step 3:

Pour the cream, the rest of the sugar, and vanilla extract into a mixing bowl. Whisk the mixture until it forms soft peaks.

Step 4:

Break the sponge cake or brownies into large chunks and add to the cream with the strawberry puree.

Step 5:

Using a wooden spoon, gently stir the cake and strawberry puree into the whipped cream until it makes a ripple effect.

Step 6:

Spoon the cream mixture into 4 sundae dishes or bowls, then spoon over the rest of the strawberries and any juices.

marks out of 10

10=yummylicious 9=truly scrumptious
8=de-lovely 7=delicious
6=tasty 5=Mmmmmmm
4=mouthwatering 3=just nice
2=good 1=ok

Toffee banana sundae ★★

There's only one way to describe this dessert—mmmmm! It's so delicious, it
would make a great birthday treat—especially decorated with a chocolate curl
or piece of fudge.

Serves 3

prep: 15 minutes

cooking:
10 minutes

What you need:

1/3 cup Syrup

2 tbsp Superfine Sugar

2 tbsp light brown Sugar

3 tbsp butter, cut into cubes

5 tbsp heavy cream

12 pecan nuts, halved (optional)

3 large bananas, peeled and sliced

9 scoops ice cream

Equipment:

• Small Saucepan

• wooden Spoon

• Skillet

• ice-cream Scoop

Step 1:

Put the syrup, superfine sugar, brown sugar, and butter in a small saucepan. Stir to mix together and bring to a boil.

Step 2:

Let the syrup mixture bubble away for 5 minutes, until slightly thickened, carefully stirring occasionally.

Step 3:

Let the syrup mixture cool slightly in the pan, then stir in the cream to make a toffee sauce.

Step 4:

Put the pecans (if using) in a dry skillet and heat for 3 minutes, until slightly toasted. Set the nuts aside to cool.

Step 5:

Divide two-thirds of the banana between 3 sundae dishes or bowls, then add 2 scoops of ice cream to each dish and a few pecans, if using.

Step 6:

Drizzle over a spoonful of the toffee sauce and top with another scoop of ice cream, the nuts, remaining banana, and some more sauce.

marks out of 10

10=yummylicious 9=truly scrumptious
8=de-lovely 7=delicious
6=tasty 5=Mmmmmmm
4=mouthwatering 3=just nice
2=good 1=ok

. . . .

Chocolate sparkles ★★

These creamy milk chocolate truffles make the perfect gift. Try presenting them in a clear bag, brightened up with a colorful ribbon, or a small gift box. Cake decorations make colorful coatings, so check out your favorites.

Makes about 5

prep: 25 minutes,
plus chilling

cooking:
5 minutes

What you need:

10½ oz/300 g good-quality
   milk chocolate

scant ½ cup heavy cream

1 tsp vanilla extract

1 tbsp confectioners' sugar

1½-2 tbsp butter

To decorate:

sprinkles; silver or pink stars;
   grated or flaked white chocolate,
   or your favorite decorations

Equipment:

• heatproof mixing bowl

• medium-size saucepan

• spatula

• oven mitts

• teaspoon

• small paper liners

Step 1:

Break the chocolate into even-size pieces and put it in a heatproof bowl with the cream.

Step 2: (!)

Put the bowl over a saucepan containing about 1 inch/2.5 cm of water—make sure the bowl rests on top and doesn't touch the water.

Step 3: (!)

Heat the water—but do not let it boil—and gently melt the chocolate, stirring occasionally to mix it with the cream.

Step 4: (!)

Using oven mitts, remove the bowl from the pan and let cool slightly. Stir in the vanilla extract, confectioners' sugar, and butter until mixed in.

Step 5:

Chill until the mixture is firm. Use a teaspoon to scoop up some of the mixture, then roll into a ball shape. Repeat until the mixture is used up.

Step 6:

Dip the chocolate balls into your favorite coatings, turning them until they are evenly coated. Arrange the chocolates in small paper liners.

marks out of 10

10=yummylicious **9**=truly scrumptious
8=de-lovely **7**=delicious
6=tasty **5**=Mmmmmmm
4=mouthwatering **3**=just nice
2=good **1**=ok

. . . .

Flower and bug cupcakes**

Making and decorating your own cupcakes is plenty of fun. Experiment with different colored icing and cake decorations to create your own versions of these flower and bug cakes.

Makes 12

prep: 10 minutes

cooking:
15–20 minutes

What you need:

1¼ cups self-rising flour

1 tsp baking powder

heaping ¾ cup superfine sugar

¾ cup soft unsalted butter, cut
   into small pieces

3 eggs at room temperature

1 tsp vanilla extract

2 tbsp milk

Decoration:

1 ¾ cups confectioners' sugar

1 tbsp lemon juice

1–2 tbsp water

few drops of blue and green
   food coloring

white chocolate candies

chocolate candies with sprinkles

gummy candy bugs

Equipment:

• large paper or plastic liners

• muffin pan

• large mixing bowl

• handheld electric mixer

• wooden spoon

• metal spoons

• wire cooling rack

Step 1: ❗

Turn the oven on to 350°F/180°C. Put 12 paper liners into a muffin pan. Sift the flour, baking powder, and superfine sugar into a bowl.

Step 2: ❗

Add the butter, eggs, vanilla extract, and milk. Use a handheld electric mixer or wooden spoon to make a smooth creamy mixture.

Step 3: ❗

Divide the cake mixture between the paper liners. Bake for 15–20 minutes, until risen and golden. Cool on a wire rack.

Step 4:

Mix together the confectioners' sugar, lemon juice, and water to make a smooth icing. Color half of the icing blue and half of the icing green.

Step 5:

Spread the icing over the cakes. For flower cakes, place a white chocolate candy in the center and the sprinkled ones around it.

Step 6:

For bug cakes, using the green icing, pipe a leaf or blades of grass on each cake and top with a gummy candy bug.

marks out of 10

10=yummylicious **9**=truly scrumptious
8=de-lovely **7**=delicious
6=tasty **5**=Mmmmmmm
4=mouthwatering **3**=just nice
2=good **1**=ok

. . . .

Jelly cookies ★★

These golden, buttery, vanilla cookies taste similar to shortbread but have a delicious gooey jelly center. Share them with your family and friends for an afternoon treat.

Makes 15

prep: 15 minutes, plus chilling

cooking: 12 minutes

What you need:

Scant ½cup softened unsalted butter, cut into small pieces

5 tbsp superfine sugar

1 egg, lightly beaten

1 tsp vanilla extract

1 cup self-rising flour

4 tbsp cornstarch

4 tsp strawberry jelly

Equipment:

• large mixing bowl

• handheld electric mixer

• wooden spoon

• small bowl

• strainer

• 2 baking sheets

• parchment paper

• tablespoon

Step 1:

Put the butter and superfine sugar into a mixing bowl. Whisk with a handheld electric mixer or beat with a wooden spoon until light and creamy.

Step 2:

Mix together the egg and vanilla extract and add, a little at a time, to the bowl, whisking or beating until mixed in.

Step 3:

Next, sift the flour and cornstarch into the bowl and gently fold in with a wooden spoon to make a soft dough.

Step 4: !

Turn on the oven to 350°F/180°C. Line 2 baking sheets with parchment paper to prevent the cookies from sticking.

Step 5:

Take a heaped tablespoon of the mixture and form it into a ball. Repeat to make 15 balls and place them spaced apart on the baking sheets.

Step 6: !

Chill the cookies for about 15 minutes, then use your thumb to make an indent in the middle and fill with jelly. Bake for 12 minutes.

marks out of 10

10=yummylicious 9=truly scrumptious
8=de-lovely 7=delicious
6=tasty 5=Mmmmmmm
4=mouthwatering 3=just nice
2=good 1=ok

. . . .

59

My own apple pie ★★★

To make your personalized apple pies, roll out the dough and carefully cut out your initials, and those of your family. After brushing the pies with egg, stick on the letters and brush again before baking.

Makes 4

prep: 20 minutes, plus chilling

cooking: 30–35 minutes

What you need:

heaping 1½ cups all-purpose flour
pinch of salt
2 tbsp confectioners' sugar
½ cup cold unsalted butter
  (or half butter and half vegetable
  fat), cut into small pieces
1 egg, separated
1–2 tbsp cold water

Filling:

1 lb 8 oz/675 g apples, peeled,
  halved, cored, and thinly sliced
2 tbsp orange juice
1 tsp ground cinnamon
3 tbsp superfine sugar

Equipment:

• large mixing bowl
• 4 small heatproof dishes
• rolling pin
• baking sheet
• sharp knife

Step 1:

Sift the flour, salt, and confectioners' sugar into a bowl. Add the butter and rub it into the flour mixture with your fingertips.

Step 2:

When the mixture looks like fine breadcrumbs, mix in the egg yolk and water. Form the mixture into a ball with your hands.

Step 3:

Cover the pastry dough with plastic wrap and chill for 30 minutes. Mix the apple slices with the orange juice, cinnamon, and superfine sugar.

Step 4: (!)

Turn on the oven to 400°F/200°C. Divide the apple mixture between the 4 heatproof dishes. Wet the rim of each dish.

Step 5: (!)

Roll out the pastry dough and cut 4 round tops. Top each pie with a pastry circle, trim the edges, and press with a fork.

Step 6: (!)

Brush each pie with egg white and make a slit in the top; decorate as described on page 60. Put on a baking sheet and bake for 30–35 minutes.

marks out of 10

10=yummylicious **9**=truly scrumptious
8=de-lovely **7**=delicious
6=tasty **5**=Mmmmmmm
4=mouthwatering **3**=just nice
2=good **1**=ok

. . . .

Cooking words

Here are some cooking terms that you will find in this book with simple explanations:

Bake: Cook a food/dish in the oven.

Beat: Stir or mix an ingredient in order to add air.

Blend: Mix ingredients together in a food processor or blender to make a smooth mixture or liquid.

Boil: Heat a liquid, such as water, over a high heat until it bubbles.

Broil: Cook or brown food under intense heat.

Chill: Cool an ingredient or food in the refrigerator.

Chop: Cut an ingredient into smaller pieces.

Cream: Beat butter and sugar together, using a wooden spoon or food processor to add air until it is light and fluffy.

Drain: Pour off unwanted liquid, sometimes through a colander or strainer, or remove excess oil after frying by placing the food on paper towels.

Drizzle: Slowly pour a trickle of a liquid or sauce over a food.

Dry-fry: Cook ingredients, such as nuts and seeds, in a skillet without using oil.

Fold in: Mix one ingredient into another but gently, and sometimes gradually, to prevent losing any air.

Fry: Cook food in oil in a skillet or saucepan over a direct heat.

Grate: Rub food, such as cheese, vegetables, or chocolate, up and down a grater over holes of varying sizes to make thin or thick shreds.

Grease: Lightly coat a baking sheet, cake pan, or dish, using oil or butter to prevent sticking.

Juice: Extract liquid from an ingredient, such as fruit, using a squeezer or an electric juicer.

Marinade: A mixture of oil, herbs, spices, and other flavorings used to flavor a food, such as meat and fish, before cooking.

Marinate: Flavor an ingredient, such as meat or fish, by soaking it in a mixture of oil, herbs, spices, and other flavorings for a period of time.

Mash: Crush food, such as bananas or cooked potatoes, to produce a smooth end result.

Melt: Turn a solid, such as chocolate or butter, into a liquid, using heat.

Peel: Remove the skin from food, such as fruit and vegetables, using a peeler or small knife.

Puree: Blend or liquidize (usually with a little water) a food, such as fruit or vegetables, into a pulp.

Rinse: Place food under a cold running water tap.

Roll out: Flatten a food, such as pastry dough, into a smooth, even layer using a rolling pin.

Roughly chop: Cut an ingredient into pieces of varying sizes.

Rub in: Mix fat, such as butter, into flour with your fingertips until the mixture looks like fine breadcrumbs.

Season: Add flavor to food using salt and pepper.

Sift: Put an ingredient, such as flour, through a strainer to remove lumps and add air.

Simmer: Cook food gently in a pan over a low direct heat, making sure it does not boil.

Slice: Cut a food into thick or thin strips or pieces.

Stir: Mix ingredients together to combine them into one mixture and prevent sticking if being cooked.

Whisk: Quickly stir or mix an ingredient or mixture, using a fork or a kitchen utensil called a whisk, in order to add air.

Index